Chri

*B i b l e  S t u d i e s*

# STAYING FAITHFUL

## Andrea Sterk Louthan & Howard Louthan

in 6 or 12 studies
for individuals or groups

*With Notes for Leaders*

INTERVARSITY PRESS
DOWNERS GROVE, ILLINOIS 60515

InterVarsity Press is the book-publishing division of InterVarsity Christian Fellowship, a student movement active on campus at hundreds of universities, colleges and schools of nursing in the United States of America, and a member movement of the International Fellowship of Evangelical Students. For information about local and regional activities, write Public Relations Dept., InterVarsity Christian Fellowship, 6400 Schroeder Rd., P.O. Box 7895, Madison, WI 53707-7895.

All Scripture quotations, unless otherwise indicated, are taken from the HOLY BIBLE, NEW INTERNATIONAL VERSION. Copyright © 1973, 1978, 1984 International Bible Society. Used by permission of Zondervan Publishing House. All rights reserved.

Cover photograph: Robert McKendrick

ISBN 0-8308-1146-X

Printed in the United States of America ∞

| 15 | 14 | 13 | 12 | 11 | 10 | 9 | 8 | 7 | 6 | 5 | 4 | 3 |
|----|----|----|----|----|----|----|----|----|----|----|----|----|
| 03 | 02 | 01 | 00 | 99 | 98 | 97 | 96 | 95 | 94 | | | |

# Contents

## Welcome to Christian Character Bible Studies

What is a Christian character? And how does one go about developing it?

As with most questions of faith and the practice of faith, the best source of information is the Bible itself. The Christian Character Bible Studies explore a wide variety of biblical passages that speak of character development.

The Bible speaks of love—love for ourselves, love for God, love for other believers, and love for those who do not yet believe.

The Bible speaks of responsibility—responsibility for the poor, responsibility for the weak, responsibility for the environment, responsibility for our assets, responsibility to work and responsibility to share our faith.

The Bible speaks of holy living—honesty, sexual purity, mental discipline, faithfulness, courage and obedience.

The Bible speaks of hope—a hope that is based on the character of God, the work of Jesus Christ, and an accurate view of our human limitations. It is a hope that says, "Residence on earth is temporary; residence in heaven is eternal."

This series of Bible study guides will help you explore, in

thought and in practice, these many facets of Christian character. But why bother? Why can't we accept ourselves the way we are? Isn't that the route to mental health?

Not entirely. We are all in transition. Each new day brings new influences on who we are. We respond—and change. With God's help, that change can be toward Christian growth.

Growing in character is satisfying. It carries with it the sense of growing in godliness—into the image that God created us to be. It carries a sense of harmony, of walking hand in hand with God. But it is not painless. Therefore these guides will constantly ask us to hold up our character to the mirror of Scripture and to bend that character along the lines of Christ's image. God doesn't want us to stay the same. We should allow the Spirit to nudge us through these studies toward the spiritual maturity that God designed for his people.

## What Kind of Guide Is This?

This is an inductive Bible study guide. That means that each study deals with a particular passage of Scripture and attempts to understand its content, its meaning, and its implications for godly living. A variety of questions will explore all three of those areas.

This is a thought-provoking guide. Each question assumes a variety of answers. Many questions do not have "right" answers, particularly questions that aim at meaning or application. Instead, the questions should inspire users to explore the passage in more depth.

This study guide is flexible—you can use it for individual study or in a group. You can vary the amount of time you take for each study, and you have various options for the number of studies you do from the guide. This is possible because every guide in this series is structured with two unique features. First, each of the six studies is divided into two parts, and second, several questions are marked with an asterisk (*), indicating that they may be

| \multicolumn{5}{c}{**Guidelines for Using the Christian Character Bible Studies**} |
|---|---|---|---|---|
| **Option** | **Type of Use** | **Time Allowed** | **Number of Sessions** | **Your Plan to Follow** |
| 1 | Individual | 30 minutes | 12 | Divide each study into two sessions, and use all the questions. |
| 2 | Individual | 45 minutes | 6 | Use one study per session, and skip questions with an asterisk (*) if time doesn't allow for them. |
| 3 | Individual | 60 minutes | 6 | Use one study per session, and use all the questions. |
| 4 | Group | 30 minutes | 12 | Divide each study into two sessions, and skip questions with an asterisk(*) if time doesn't allow for them. |
| 5 | Group | 45-60 minutes | 12 | Divide each study into two sessions, and use all the questions. |
| 6 | Group | 60 minutes | 6 | Use one study per session, and skip questions with an asterisk (*) if time doesn't allow for them. |
| 7 | Group | 90 minutes | 6 | Use one study per session, and use all the questions. |

skipped if time does not allow for them. So you can have six sessions or twelve, with varying amounts of time to fit your needs.

How do you decide which approach is best for you? Looking at the chart on page 6, decide if you will be using this guide for individual study or in a group. Then determine how much time you want to spend on each session and how many sessions you want to have. Then follow the plan described in the far right column.

For example, if you are using this guide in a group, you can choose from options 4, 5, 6 or 7. If you have 45-60 minutes for study and discussion in each group meeting, then you can use option 5. Or if you have only 30 minutes available, you can use option 4. These options allow you to have twelve meetings by breaking at the dividing point in each session and using all the questions, including those with an asterisk.

If your group has only six meeting times available, then follow the column headed "Number of Sessions" down to options 6 and 7. Option 6 provides for 60-minute sessions without the asterisked questions while option 6 allows for 90-minute sessions using all the questions.

Note that there are four plans that allow for in-depth study—options 1, 3, 5 and 7. These use each of the questions and will allow for the most thorough examination of Scripture and of ourselves.

With seven different options available to you, Christian Character Bible Studies offer maximum flexibility to suit your schedule and needs.

Each study is composed of three sections: an introduction with a question of approach to the topic of the day, questions that invite study of the passage or passages, and leader's notes at the back of the book. The section of questions provides space for writing observations, either in preparation for the study or during the course of the discussion. This space can form a permanent record of your thoughts and spiritual progress.

## Suggestions for Individual Study

**1.** Read the introduction. Consider the opening question, and make notes about your responses to it.

**2.** Pray, asking God to speak to you from his Word about this particular topic.

**3.** Read the passage in a modern translation of the Bible, marking phrases that seem important. Note in the margin any questions that come to your mind as you read.

**4.** Use the questions from the study guide to more thoroughly examine the passage. (Questions are phrased from the New International Version of the Bible.) Note your findings in the space provided. After you have made your own notes, read the corresponding leader's notes in the back of the book for further insights. (You can ignore the comments about moderating the dynamics of a discussion group.) Consult the bibliography for further information.

**5.** Re-read the entire passage, making further notes about its general principles and about the personal use you intend to make of them.

**6.** Pray. Speak to God about insights you have gained into his character—and your own. Tell him of any desires you have for specific growth. Ask his help as you attempt to live out the principles described in that passage.

## Suggestions for Group Study

Joining a Bible study group can be a great avenue to spiritual growth. Here are a few guidelines that will help you as you participate in the studies in this guide.

**1.** These are inductive Bible studies. That means that you will discuss a particular passage of Scripture—in-depth. Only rarely should you refer to other portions of the Bible, and then only at the request of the leader. Of course, the Bible is internally consistent, and other good forms of study draw on that consistency, but inductive Bible study sticks with a single passage and works on it in-depth.

**2.** These are discussion studies. Questions in this guide aim at helping a group discuss together a passage of Scripture in order to understand its content, meaning and implications. Most people are either natural talkers or natural listeners. Yet this type of study works best if people participate more or less evenly. Try to curb any natural tendency to either excessive talking or excessive quiet. You and the rest of the group will benefit.

**3.** Most questions in this guide invite a variety of answers. If you disagree with someone else's comment, say so (kindly). Then explain your own point-of-view from the passage before you.

**4.** Be willing to lead a discussion. Much of the preparation for leading has already been accomplished in the writing of this guide. If you have observed someone else direct the discussion two or three times, you are probably ready to lead.

**5.** Respect the privacy of others in your group. Many people speak of things within the context of a Bible study/prayer group, that they do not want as public knowledge. Assume that personal information spoken within the group setting is private, unless you are specifically told otherwise. And don't talk about it elsewhere.

**6.** Enjoy your study. Prepare to grow. God bless.

### Suggestions for Group Leaders

Specific suggestions to help you appear in the leader's notes at the back of this guide. Read the opening section of the leader's notes carefully, even if you are only leading one group meeting. Then you can go to the section on the particular study you will lead.

# Introducing Staying Faithful

One of the most compelling human needs is acceptance.

From childhood through retirement, we try in different ways to fit in with a group. Within a year a teenager may run through half a dozen fads in order to gain the approval of his or her peers. No less susceptible to peer pressure, working men and women alter their behavior or modify their opinions to win the favor of their colleagues. Even grandparents sometimes attempt to buy the love and acceptance of their grandchildren by showering them with gifts.

If left unchecked, the longing to be accepted can seduce us. We may find ourselves advocating views or engaging in activities which we at one time considered unhealthy. Before long our values and even our identity may be subtly undermined by the tendency to conform to those around us.

In some societies the pressure to conform is even greater. In totalitarian regimes failure to do what is expected may have serious consequences. And yet here we often find the most striking examples of individuals who refuse to sacrifice their identity on the altar of public approval. From Aleksandr Solzhenitsyn to Nelson Mandela, they remind us of what it means to stay faithful to one's convictions and values in even the most oppressive circumstances.

One of the most prominent prisoners of conscience in recent years is Vaclav Havel. Formerly a playwright, Havel was harassed and imprisoned several times for daring to speak out against the communist government of Czechoslovakia. Having won the acclaim of his people by his integrity, in the Velvet Revolution of 1989 Havel rose to the presidency of the new Czechoslovak state.

Long before he came to power, Havel wrote "The Power of the Powerless," an essay about the need for personal integrity in the face of hostile circumstances. Havel tells the story of the manager of a small vegetable store, a typical working man in what was once communist Czechoslovakia.

Every day this grocer places in his display window a sign with the words "Workers of the World Unite." Neither he nor his customers ever think about the significance of this slogan. Nonetheless, the grocer was given this sign by the authorities and has hung it in the window for years just as all his fellow grocers have done. Were he not to do so, he might be reproached or ostracized. Even his livelihood might be at stake. So he continues to "play the game" to ensure a relatively peaceful life in harmony with society.

One day, however, the grocer rebels. He stops displaying the sign. In so doing he rejects the meaningless ritual imposed on him by his society. By refusing to "play the game" he steps out of what Havel calls "life in the lie." Though his rebellion may be costly, he finds again his oppressed identity, value and freedom. Through his example of "living in the truth," he exposes the deception of his society and refuses to hide his identity behind a façade of lies.

While Havel's grocer lives under a totalitarian regime, many Christians today face challenges of a different dimension. We live in a culture of relativity which has risks of its own. In a society where absolutes are denied, any assertion of absolute truth or meaning is likely to provoke a hostile response. Staying faithful to Christ in such an environment is costly.

Yielding to the pressures to conform, however, results in far more serious consequences. We end up living a lie and betraying our identity in Christ. Yet, like Havel's grocer, we can demonstrate that life in the truth is possible. By choosing truth not only do we maintain our integrity as Christ's disciples, but we also undermine the world's system which is built on lies, for when one begins to live in the truth, the meaninglessness of life in the lie is exposed.

We today are confronted almost on a daily basis with lies that threaten our identity as Christians. From the seduction of affluence to New Age promises of self-fulfillment, our society attempts to woo us with empty slogans.

Are ethical standards violated where we work or study while everyone pretends that morality is being upheld? Do we subtly appropriate habits or practices to win the acceptance of our peers? When our society feeds us lies, we can either succumb or choose to be a "dissident" by remaining true to our Christian convictions. What does our faith mean in the midst of such tensions? Do we choose to live differently because we follow Christ?

The purpose of this guide is to help us to confront these issues. The first study is an introduction to the whole theme of Christian identity, examining ways in which we are pressured to compromise our convictions and what it means to stand firm. The remaining studies focus on different aspects of living as a disciple of Christ.

"Wholehearted Commitment" presents the seriousness of following Jesus and the dangers of half-hearted devotion. "Struggling with the World's Values" helps us grapple with the challenges of living in a world of injustice and false values. In a society which is fascinated with novelty and change, the study on perseverance considers what it entails to hold fast to one's faith and commitment over the long haul. "Taking Risks" reminds us that an important part of being Christ's disciple is having the courage to follow him in new directions and in intimidating circumstances. Since all these aspects of following Christ must be undergirded by a consistent lifestyle, the final study on faithfulness calls us to be wise and responsible stewards of the resources he has entrusted to us.

It is our hope that these studies will encourage you to remain faithful, holding fast as a follower of Christ in even the most challenging circumstances.

*Andrea and Howard Louthan*

# ONE

## *IDENTITY*

*2 Kings 18:17-37; 19:1-19*

Our society is locked in a longstanding identity crisis. From the troubled teen years beset with self-image problems to the midlife crisis and beyond many of those around us do not know who they are.

The community of believers is supposed to be different. Pulpits across the country proclaim that our identity is rooted and grounded in Jesus Christ. But after the Sunday message many Christians walk out into the world only to sink back into the quagmire of their own identity crisis.

We shouldn't be surprised that so many of us wrestle with this problem. God's Word makes it clear that his people live in a halfway house between heaven and hell, adherents to God's truth within a world of lies.

These two cultures are on a collision course, and every day there are situations where we as Christians are challenged by the society in which we live. Sometimes our culture intimidates us and attempts to erode confidence in our identity as God's people.

The following passage from 2 Kings gives one such example. Besieging Jerusalem with a powerful army, the Assyrian King Sennacherib issues a threat not only to King Hezekiah and the kingdom of Judah but also a direct challenge to the entire identity of God's people.

## Part One

1. How might our media and culture provoke an identity crisis in the life of a Christian?

**Read 2 Kings 18:17-37.**

2. Describe the threat facing Hezekiah and the people of Judah.

3. Speaking through the field commander, Sennacherib, the king of Assyria, addresses Hezekiah and his assistants. What kinds of questions does Sennacherib raise in verses 19-20?

4. How does Sennacherib try to shake Judah's confidence in verses 21-24?

*5. What tactic does he use in verse 25?

*How might this approach have affected the listeners?

*6. Why do Hezekiah's administrators ask the field commander to speak in Aramaic (v. 26)?

*What does this suggest about the mood of the city?

7. Compare Hezekiah's exhortation (v. 30) with the offer of the king of Assyria (vv. 31-33). What are the relative benefits of these two appeals?

8. In what sense does the king of Assyria attempt to undermine their identity as God's chosen people (vv. 33-35)?

9. What tactics does our culture use to cause us to question our identity as God's people?

10. In what aspect of your identity do you feel particularly vulnerable to attack?

*What would it mean for you to "trust in the Lord" (v. 30) in responding to this threat?

**Part Two**
*11. How do you tend to feel and respond when your faith or confidence in God is tested?

**Read 2 Kings 19:1-19.**
12. Describe Hezekiah's attitude and actions in response to the ominous words of the king (vv. 1-4).

*13. How does Hezekiah assess the situation, and what request does he make of Isaiah (vv. 3-4)?

14. Compare Sennacherib's view of God and the Assyrian army (vv. 9-13) with the picture presented in Isaiah's prophecy (vv. 6-7). How do they differ?

*15. In what way does today's society define our identity in a different manner than God?

**\*16.** How might two such conflicting views of reality challenge you in everyday life? Give an example from your own experience.

**17.** Confronted with his own crisis, Hezekiah brings his dilemma before the Lord. Reread verses 3-4 and Hezekiah's prayer in verses 15-19. How has Hezekiah's perception changed?

**18.** Review Sennacherib's boasts in verses 10-13. How does Hezekiah now evaluate Sennacherib's claims (vv. 17-18)?

**19.** In what ways does Hezekiah's recognition of God's true nature affect his view of himself and the situation around him?

**20.** What can we learn from Hezekiah's example about confronting the lies the world feeds us?

**\*21.** How would a reaffirmation of God's character be of help when we face overt or subtle attacks on our identity as Christians?

*optional question

# TWO

## WHOLEHEARTED COMMITMENT

*Acts 4:32—5:11*

*O*f all the world's religions Christianity claims the largest following. Millions of people throughout the world consider themselves Christians. For some this means only a visit to church on Christmas and Easter, while in other societies following Christ can cost people their job or even their life. Clearly Christians define commitment in various ways.

Perhaps part of the problem is a misunderstanding of God's grace. While Christians acknowledge that they are "saved by grace," many fall prey to what Dietrich Bonhoeffer, the twentieth-century German theologian, called "cheap grace." People focus on the benefits of Christ's redemptive work without taking seriously the cost of commitment.

In an age where many Christians live by "cheap grace," Bonhoeffer himself furnishes a striking example of wholehearted commitment to the Lord Jesus. Refusing to flee Nazi Germany, he ministered to the underground Christian church which resisted

Hitler's regime. Eventually, his devotion to Christ led to his imprisonment and execution.

Many of us associate the early church with zeal and sacrificial service. Yet here too, different levels of commitment are evident. This study contrasts two first-century views of what it meant to follow Christ—"cheap grace" versus wholehearted commitment.

## Part One

**1.** If someone were to describe your church or fellowship group, what adjectives might he or she use?

**Read Acts 4:32-35.**
**2.** What phrases does Luke use to portray the character of the early church?

**3.** In what way does verse 32 demonstrate the believers' obedience to the two great commandments—love of God and love of one's neighbor?

**4.** In verses 33-35 we see the apostles involved in two types of ministry. What kind of ministry is described in verse 33?

**\*5.** How does the apostles' ministry in this verse compare with your own?

6. Note the other task the apostles are engaged in (vv. 34-35). What is the significance of their involvement in two very different types of ministry?

*7. How does the ministry of your church or fellowship group compare with the early church's dual commitment to meeting spiritual and practical needs?

What steps could your group make to maintain a balance between these two aspects of commitment?

8. How is the believers' commitment to Christ demonstrated in their lifestyle and what is the result?

**Read Acts 4:36-37.**
9. What do we find out about Barnabas in these verses?

What do you think motivates him in his business dealings?

**10.** What is distinctive about your way of living because you are committed to Christ?

What areas of your life could better reflect your devotion to the Lord?

**Part Two**
**\*11.** Think of a Christian whose commitment you admire. Describe his or her outstanding characteristics.

In Acts 4:32-35 Luke introduces us to the church's way of life. In 4:36-37 he provides a positive example of giving to the church through Barnabas. In 5:1-11 we see a negative example of this pattern.

**Read Acts 5:1-11.**
**12.** Describe the deceptive ploy orchestrated by Ananias and Sapphira.

What role did each of them play?

**13.** What was the result of their offense for themselves and for the church as a whole (vv. 5, 11)?

Why was their sin so serious?

**14.** Can you think of ways in which you have been holding back or less than wholehearted in your relationship with God? Explain.

***15.** What was the significance of the fact that donations to the church were offered on a voluntary basis?

***16.** What does this story teach us about God?

about integrity?

**17.** Barnabas and Ananias and Sapphira sold property and gave proceeds to the church. In light of their respective actions, in what different ways do you think they would define Christian commitment?

***18.** In what ways do Christians today tend to minimize the call to commitment?

**19.** What would it mean in your own life to "sell a field" for the sake of your church or fellowship group?

*optional question

# THREE

## STRUGGLING WITH THE WORLD'S VALUES

*Psalm 73*

*H*ave you ever been frustrated by the prosperity of the un-
godly or by blatant injustice in the world? Perhaps you've felt at
times that upholding Christian values has simply not paid off in a
world in which ambition, status and power are valued and even
rewarded.

If you've struggled with such feelings, you're in good company.
In various ways, these issues plagued the hearts and minds of biblical figures like Jeremiah, Job and Elijah, as well as St. Augustine
and a whole host of godly men and women throughout the history
of the church.

Many people in our world value power, fame, wealth and physical
appearance. In contrast, as Christians we are committed to One
who came in weakness and humility, was born in relative obscurity,
was rejected by his own people, and died a shameful death well
before reaching what most would consider his prime. Yet as we
come to worship him, our perspective is radically transformed, and

our values are realigned. In the midst of a morally bankrupt world, we reaffirm our commitment to follow Jesus.

Today's passage recounts the spiritual journey of another man who struggled with similar issues. He was a musician, the director of the temple choir, and a Levite. What Asaph describes in Psalm 73 is his journey from disillusionment and despair to a discovery of truth and to ultimate delight in the presence of a loving God.

**Part One**

1. Relate one incident that caused you to be frustrated by the apparent injustice of the world.

**Read Psalm 73:1-14.**

2. How does the psalmist's tone change after verse 1?

3. According to Asaph, what lay at the root of his frustration?

*4. What is the difference between being angry at injustice and being envious of those who benefit from it?

5. In verses 4-9 Asaph provides a detailed description of "the wicked." What positive characteristics does he attribute to them (vv. 4-5)?

**6.** List the negative attributes of the wicked in verses 6-9.

**\*7.** What is Asaph's complaint in verse 10?

**8.** How do you feel when you see "wicked" (arrogant or malicious) people prospering financially or gaining esteem in the eyes of those around them?

**\*9.** In what sense does God factor into the thinking of "the wicked" (v. 11)?

**\*10.** Describe Asaph's emotions in verses 13-14.

**11.** Have you ever felt that your efforts to live for Christ have been in vain? Explain.

**12.** Given Asaph's perception of the world in the rest of the passage, why do you think he began the psalm with a positive statement about God?

*13. Think of a difficult situation you face. What can you affirm about God which enables you to trust him despite the adverse circumstances you are in?

**Part Two**
*14. How have you dealt with doubt or depression in your life as a Christian?

**Read Psalm 73:15-28.**
15. In verse 15 how has Asaph's focus changed?

*16. When do you think it might be wise to be careful in expressing your doubts? Why?

17. Where does Asaph finally find an answer to his dilemma (v. 17)? Why is this significant?

*18. How can worship change our perspective on a situation which is oppressing us?

**19.** What is the psalmist's new view of "the wicked" (vv. 18-20)?

**20.** What does Asaph see as the cause of his earlier disillusionment with God's goodness (vv. 21-22)?

**21.** How has his earlier lament in verse 9 been transformed by his new realization of what he possesses in God (vv. 25-26)?

**22.** Describe Asaph's final assessment of his own situation and of those whom he once envied.

**23.** Which aspect of Asaph's spiritual journey is most helpful for you in your own struggle with the values of the world? Why?

*optional question

# FOUR

## *PERSEVERANCE*

*Hebrews 10:19-39*

*T*he information age we live in has had a curious effect on our culture. With the microchip and the computer has come an astonishing array of products which threaten to overwhelm us. From the newest high-tech tennis rackets to the latest modifications on compact disc players our society seems to thrive on novelty and change. It's hard to be satisfied with the old black-and-white TV when the neighbors down the street have cable, color and a wall-sized screen.

There are times when we struggle with this type of thinking in our Christian lives. After years of following Christ, the original excitement we experienced as Christians sometimes fades. Different values or interests may gradually lure us away from our commitment.

Even if we manage to resist the temptation of succumbing to the world's pressures, we often end up viewing the Christian life in a somewhat negative light. We may see it as an individual struggle to hold on to our faith in the face of subtle enticements, persistent attacks and the defections of others.

The writer of Hebrews presents a different perspective on per-severance in the Christian life. It is not an individual struggle against ever-increasing difficulties, but a communal pilgrimage. It is a call to support and encourage one another as we move ahead in our faith upheld by the strength and gracious presence of the Lord himself.

**Part One**

**1.** Some people who set out to follow Christ seem to gradually fall away from their commitment. Why do you think this happens?

**Read Hebrews 10:19-31.**
**2.** On what grounds are the Hebrews encouraged to enter God's presence with confidence in verses 19-21?

**\*3.** Notice the language used in these verses: "Most Holy Place," "a new and living way," and "a great priest." Why do you think the author has chosen this way of describing our approach to God?

**4.** What does verse 22 teach us about how we should approach God?

**5.** How does our nearness to God relate to the three commands given in verses 23-25?

*6. Why do you think the writer mentions God's faithfulness in his exhortation to persevere?

7. How and why does the author link community with perseverance in verses 24-25?

*8. Have you seen this relationship in your own experience? Explain.

*9. In the context of this call to persevere what is the significance of the final phrase of verse 25?

10. In what sense are the warnings in verses 26-31 related to the exhortations in verses 19-25?

*11. Verse 26 describes people who have come to a knowledge of the truth, yet "deliberately keep on sinning." Why do you think someone would do this?

12. This passage contrasts two lifestyles—persevering in faith and persisting in sin. What practical steps could you take to pursue the former and avoid the latter?

How could you help a brother or sister in this same challenge?

**Part Two**
***13.** Why do new Christians often seem to be more excited about following Christ than do older believers?

**Read Hebrews 10:32-39.**
**14.** How does the author characterize the Hebrew Christians as new believers?

***15.** Why do you think these young Christians were able to endure such hardship and persecution?

**16.** What hardships do you or Christians you know face because of your efforts to live for Christ?

***17.** How could you stand "side by side" with those who encounter persecution?

**18.** What motivations for perseverance does the writer provide in verses 35-37?

**19.** What does the author's use of the two Old Testament passages in verses 37-38 suggest about the connection between Christ's return and a life of faith?

**20.** How do the writer's final words of encouragement relate to the stern warnings of verses 26-31 and affirm the identity of the Hebrew Christians?

**\*21.** Judging from this passage would you characterize perseverance as an active or passive trait? Explain.

**22.** In this passage the author appeals to both the past and the future to motivate the Hebrew Christians to continue steadfastly in their walk with Christ. How could reflections on your own past or thoughts of the future serve as an encouragement to persevere?

**23.** How might your perseverance through difficult circumstances encourage others to stand firm in their identity as Christians?

\*optional question

# FIVE

## *TAKING RISKS*

*Numbers 13:1—14:9*

*H*istory has shown us that, whether capitalist, communist or somewhere in between, all societies inevitably drift toward conservatism. Whether recalling the past or following proud traditions, our culture is hesitant to break from its heritage in any way. Those who challenge society's standards risk disapproval or even ostracism.

We are constantly warned about the folly of taking risks. From life insurance to safe long-term investments, we are encouraged to save and conserve our resources. While this might be prudent financial advice, it can have a dangerous trickle-down effect in the lives of Christians.

We tend to adapt all too easily to a safe and comfortable lifestyle. In our walk with Christ we often follow the path of least resistance, avoiding challenges which intimidate us. We accept our Savior by faith, but all too quickly we begin to walk by sight.

Today's passage reminds us that an essential element of faithfulness to Christ is the willingness to risk. On the threshold of the promised land the children of Israel are faced with a critical choice. They can opt for the path of least resistance or dare to trust their God.

## Part One

1. What aspect of following Christ frightens or challenges you the most?

## Read Numbers 13:1-33.

2. What task does the Lord set before Moses (vv. 1-2)?

What promise accompanies his command?

3. What kind of information does Moses ask the Israelite leaders to gather (vv. 18-20)?

*4. Give a quick summary of their reconnaissance mission (vv. 21-25).

5. What negative and positive aspects of the land do the spies describe in their report to the Israelite community (vv. 27-29)?

*6. How do you think the Israelites initially reacted to this information (v. 30)?

*7. How do you normally respond in the face of menacing circumstances?

8. What specific concerns do the spies express to the Israelites in verses 31-33?

9. How does the information they add in these verses exceed the report they were commissioned to give?

10. How does Caleb's perception of the situation (v. 30) contrast with that of the other spies?

Why do you think they have such different perspectives on the same situation?

*11. Think of a specific situation when you felt intimidated by the circumstances God had placed you in. How did this challenge affect your relationship with God?

**12.** The spies were overwhelmed by the greater size and strength of the giant Nephilim. What would it mean for you to adopt Caleb's perspective as you struggle with a "giant" in your own life?

**Part Two**
***13.** How would you characterize most people you know with regard to facing personal challenges? (Are they bold—ready to take risks? Or do they play it safe—generally preserving the status quo?)

Why do you think this is so?

**Read Numbers 14:1-9.**
**14.** Describe the atmosphere in the camp.

***15.** How do the Israelites respond to the conflicting assessments of the land the spies have explored (vv. 1-4)?

**16.** What is the significance of their desire to return to Egypt?

**17.** In your Christian experience have you ever reached a point when you wanted to "go back to Egypt"? Explain.

**\*18.** How might you have expected the Israelite leaders to respond to the complaints of their people?

**19.** What is surprising about the reactions of Moses, Aaron, Joshua and Caleb (vv. 5-6)?

**20.** Compare Caleb and Joshua's perception of the land's inhabitants (v. 9) with that of the other spies (13:31).

**21.** What do Caleb and Joshua remind the people about their identity (vv. 8-9)?

How should this affect their perspective on taking the land?

**22.** In verse 10 the people respond to Moses, Aaron, Joshua and Caleb by talking about stoning them. Clearly, their stance for God had put them in physical danger. What type of risks might Christians in your situation face by trusting God despite the opposition of a majority?

**23.** In what ways are you preserving the status quo in your Christian life?

Where might God be calling you to step out in faith in a risky situation?

*optional question

# SIX

## FAITHFULNESS

*Matthew 25:14-46*

While the 1960s marked an era of stylish poverty and social activism, the next two decades ushered in a new wave of affluence and consumerism. Anti-war fervor was traded in for a zeal of a different kind. Financial investments, high-paying jobs and an unquenchable thirst for bigger houses, better cars and more material possessions became the pressing concern.

Unfortunately, much of this consumer mentality has carried over into the Christian community. Church building projects are spiraling out of control. We go to more and more conferences and accumulate more Christian books. Even on a spiritual level we are troubled by those gifts and resources we *don't* have. We seem to think that if we only had a certain gift or more money to give, then we could serve Christ more faithfully.

The essence of faithfulness, however, is using what we *do* have for Christ's sake. Not only has Christ entrusted us with the Gospel and various spiritual gifts, but he has also placed us in specific

settings where we have the opportunity to serve.
In the following passage Jesus tells two parables which illustrate the meaning of faithfulness. They encourage us to identify the resources God has entrusted to us and challenge us to use them more faithfully.

**Part One**
1. Why do people invest money?

In what other areas of life do people make investments?

**Read Matthew 25:14-30.**
2. What task does the master entrust to his servants? Why?

*3. On what basis does the master allot funds?

4. How does each servant handle the money that has been entrusted to him (vv. 16-18)?

5. What do we learn about faithfulness from the master's response to the first two servants (vv. 19-23)?

*6. What does this tell us about the character of the master?

7. What do the third servant's actions suggest about his view of his master?

his understanding of faithfulness?

8. How does the master respond to the excuse of the third servant (vv. 24-27, 30)?

*9. Why do you think he reacts so harshly?

10. What kinds of excuses do Christians make today for not using the gifts and abilities entrusted to them?

11. What does the master do for the first two servants in verses 28-29? Why?

**\*12.** What "talents" has God given to you?

**13.** To what extent are you investing the gifts God has given you as the first two servants did?

**Part Two**

**\*14.** The passage we are studying today emphasizes one aspect of the relationship between faith and good works, an issue which has been debated in the church for 2,000 years. How would you describe the connection between them?

**Read Matthew 25:31-46.**

**15.** What is the setting of this passage?

**16.** On what basis are the sheep judged? (How are they described? How is their faithfulness rewarded?)

**17.** What judgment is passed on the goats and why?

**\*18.** What does this teach us concerning the sin of omission?

**19.** Compare the responses of the righteous (sheep) and the unrighteous (goats) (vv. 37-39, 44). What different attitudes lie behind the questions they raise?

**20.** How does the king reply to the questions of the sheep and the goats (vv. 40, 45-46)?

**\*21.** What does his response suggest about "the least of these"?

**\*22.** Reflecting on both sections of Matthew 25, describe the relationship between faith and faithfulness in the Christian life.

**23.** What would it mean for you to be faithful in serving the needy people Christ has placed around you?

**\*24.** What one step could you take this week to apply the lesson taught here by Jesus?

*optional question

# Leader's Notes

Leading a Bible discussion can be an enjoyable and rewarding experience. But it can also be intimidating—especially if you've never done it before. If this is how you feel, you're in good company. When God asked Moses to lead the Israelites out of Egypt, he replied, "O Lord, please send someone else to do it!" (Ex 4:13). But God's response to all of his servants—including you—is essentially the same: "My grace is sufficient for you" (2 Cor 12:9).

There is another reason you should feel encouraged. Leading a Bible discussion is not difficult if you follow certain guidelines. You don't need to be an expert on the Bible or a trained teacher. The suggestions listed below should enable you to effectively and enjoyably fulfill your role as leader. And remember the discussion leader usually learns the most—so lead and grow!

### Preparing for the Study

Group leaders can prepare to lead a group by following much the same pattern outlined for individual study at the beginning of this guide. Try to begin preparation far enough in advance for the Spirit of God to begin to use the passage in your own life. Then you will have some idea about what group members will experience as they attempt to live out the passage. Advance preparation will also give your mind time to thoughtfully consider the concepts—probably in odd moments when you least expect it.

Study the flow of the questions. Consider the time available. Plan for an appropriate break (if you are using two sessions) and which optional questions you will use. Note this in your study guide so that you will not feel lost in the middle of the discussion. But be ready to make changes "en route" if the pattern of discussion demands it. Pencil near the questions any information from the leader's section that you don't want to forget. This will eliminate clumsy page turns in the middle of the discussion.

And pray. Pray for each person in the group—by name. Ask that God will prepare that person, just as he is preparing you, to confront the truths of this passage of his Word.

### During the Study

**1.** One of the major jobs of the discussion leader is to pace the study. Don't make your job more difficult by beginning late. So keep an eye on the clock. When the agreed time to begin arrives, launch the study.

**2.** Take appropriate note of the introductory essay, then ask the approach question. Encourage each of the group members to respond to the question. When everyone is involved in discussing the general topic of the day, you are ready to explore the Scripture.

**3.** Read the passage aloud, or ask others to read aloud—by paragraphs, not verses. Verse-by-verse reading breaks the flow of thought and reduces understanding. And silent reading often makes concentration difficult, especially for people who are distracted by small noises or who are uncomfortable with group silence. So read aloud—by paragraphs.

**4.** Keep in mind that the leader's job is to help a group to discover together the content, meaning and implications of a passage of Scripture. People should focus on each other and on the Bible—not necessarily on you. Your job is to moderate a discussion, to keep conversation from lagging, to draw in quiet members, and to pace the study. So encourage multiple responses to questions, and encourage people to interact with each other's observations. Volunteer your own answers only in similar proportion to others in the group.

**5.** Pacing is a major difficulty for inexperienced leaders. Most group participants have set obligations after a scheduled Bible study. You will earn their thanks if you close the study at a predictable time. But to do so you don't want to race ahead and miss details in the early questions; nor do you want to play catch-up at the end: skipping sections people most want to talk about. Try writing in your study guide the time that you hope to finish questions at various points in the study. This will help you keep a steady pace. Note also any optional questions that you can add or subtract, depending on the pace of the study. But be alert to particular needs and interests in the group. Sometimes you should abandon even the best-laid plans in order to tend to these.

**6.** If possible, spend time talking about personal needs and praying together. Many groups begin or end by speaking of various worries, concerns, reasons for thanksgiving—or just their plans for the week. Groups who pray together often see God at work in ways far beyond their expectations. It's an excellent way to grow in faith.

**7.** If you have time, do some further reading on small groups and the dynamics of such groups. For a short, but helpful, overview read *Leading Bible Discussions* by James Nyquist and Jack Kuhatschek (InterVarsity Press). Or for a more in-depth discussion read *Small Group Leaders' Handbook* or *Good Things Come in Small Groups*, both of which are edited by Ron Nicholas (InterVarsity Press). For an excellent study of how small groups can contribute to spiritual growth read *Pilgrims in Progress* by Jim and Carol Plueddemann (Harold Shaw).

The following notes refer to specific studies in the guide:

**Study 1. Identity. 2 Kings 18:17-37; 19:1-19.**

*Purpose:* To gain a greater awareness of attempts to undermine our identity as Christians and better withstand pressure to conform to society's norms.

**Question 1.** Try to elicit a number of responses to this question from different angles. If people have trouble with it, you might show them newspaper or television advertisements which attempt to define success by the way someone looks or dresses or by what a person owns. The pressures of a working environment, academic colleagues or a peer group are other potential causes of struggle with self-image or identity.

**Question 2.** The group might benefit from the following background information: King Hezekiah of Judah, the son of Ahaz, was a zealous reformer. Earlier in 2 Kings 18 we find that the Assyrian king, Sennacherib, had conquered many of the cities of Judah. Fearing that Jerusalem itself would fall into enemy hands, Hezekiah offered Sennacherib a considerable sum of money to withdraw his army. Sennacherib accepted the bribe, but instead of retreating, he advanced against the capital city.

Keep the discussion simple here. This question should lead the group to summarize the main events of the passage. The details will be discussed in greater depth as you move through the text.

**Question 3.** The "field commander" is called "Rabshakeh" in some versions. Rabshakeh is simply the title for the Assyrian official which the NIV has translated as "field commander." Also, the NIV does not use the name Sennacherib for the king of Assyria in these verses. Should someone ask, the king is identified by that name in verse 13.

**Question 5.** In particular note the way Sennacherib adapts religious language to his own purposes. An interesting modern comparison is the way in which cults use a similar approach to win over younger or less well-grounded Christians.

**Question 6.** By his stern words of warning, the Assyrian field commander hopes to sow dissension within the besieged population of Jerusalem. Hezekiah's administrators attempt to prevent a general panic by requesting that the field commander use Aramaic and not the language of the people—Hebrew.

**Question 7.** The group should see that at least on the surface the offer of Sennacherib is much more attractive than Hezekiah's appeal to the people to "trust in the Lord." While Hezekiah promises only God's deliverance (and the king attempts to squelch even this hope), the king entices them with the promise of material prosperity for each individual. Sennacherib's tone in this passage is quite seductive.

**Question 8.** Hamath, Arpad, Sepharvaim, Hena, Ivvah and Samaria were all cities or towns captured by the Assyrians shortly before Sennacherib's reign. The reference to Samaria, the capital of the northern kingdom of Israel, would be especially disturbing to the people of Judah because of its relative proximity to Jerusalem. Also, the seizure of Samaria (c. 721 B.C.) had marked the end of the kingdom of Israel.

Here Sennacherib confuses the God of Israel with the gods of all these other cities.

**Questions 9-10.** If you are ending the study after part one, you will want to leave sufficient time to focus on these important questions of application. Try to get honest, personal responses to question 10 from a number of group members. Focus your prayer time around areas of concern that have been shared. If you are covering the whole study in one session, you may want to skip the second part of question 10.

**Question 11.** This question should help people re-enter the study of Christian identity if you are covering the study in two sessions. However, if you are doing the study in one session, you should probably leave it out since the group will have just dealt with related issues in question 10.

**Question 12.** It is important to observe that Hezekiah asked for help. So often in the Christian life we try to make it on our own through difficult or even critical situations. Hezekiah recognized his weakness and desperate need for prayer.

**Question 13.** Relevant observations may have been covered already in responses to the preceding question. If so, skip this one.

**Question 14.** See the note for question 8 with regard to some of the cities mentioned in verse 13.

**Question 16.** Help group members to consider opposing ethical standards—different notions of what is right or wrong in their workplace or among their peers. Try to get beyond generalizations. One or two specific examples would help people see the relevance of the passage to our own society.

**Question 17.** The group should note Hezekiah's fear and hesitancy in his request to Isaiah in verses 3-4 ("it may be" in v. 4) and his direct and confident prayer to the Lord in verses 15-19. His reference to "the Lord your God" (v. 3) stands in marked contrast to "O Lord our God" (v. 18). Also note his bold affirmation: "You alone are God over all the kingdoms of the earth." Hezekiah's growth in faith is striking.

You may want to point out that Isaiah's prophecy about the downfall of Sennacherib (vv. 6-7) is in fact fulfilled in verses 35-37.

**Question 18.** Hezekiah is able to distinguish the truth from the distortion of truth in Sennacherib's message (vv. 10-13). He does not dispute the destruction the Assyrians have wrought but rather the power and even the reality of their gods.

**Question 20.** This question provides a good opportunity to summarize the passage as well as to make personal application. Be sure to leave time to consider concrete steps that might be taken to help us stand firm as God's people—even in the midst of a hostile environment. Try to get everyone involved in the discussion.

### Study 2. Wholehearted Commitment. Acts 4:32—5:11.

*Purpose:* To understand the seriousness of Christ's call to commitment and to become more sincere and wholehearted in following him.

**Question 1.** If you are doing this study in one session you may want to consider using question 11 in place of this one as the introductory question. Question 1 helps people to think about the church or their Christian fellowship group as a whole. Question 11 focuses attention on the character of individuals. Either would provide an appropriate introduction to the whole passage.

**Question 2.** Keep the discussion general here, noting only important words and phrases. Later questions will draw out more of the
details of the passage. Notice in particular Luke's use of emphatic
words such as "no," "all" and "everything."

**Question 3.** The great commandment is found in Mark 12:30-31.
While there is no explicit mention of love of God in this verse,
oneness of heart and mind seems to refer to their common faith and
commitment to Christ.

**Questions 4-5.** Make sure the group sees both the type of ministry
(evangelism) and the way they carried it out (with great power,
perseverance, and the enjoyment of the Lord's grace).

**Question 6.** The nature of the apostles' ministry in these verses
may have already been noted in response to question 4. Be sure,
however, that the group discusses the *significance* of this ministry.
Luke includes the practical task of administering church funds
alongside evangelism in his description of the early church. The
group should recognize that there are no "unspiritual" ministries in
the body of Christ. Wholehearted commitment to Christ engages
all our resources for his service.

**Question 8.** Don't let the discussion go too far off-course debating
whether or not the early church practiced a form of proto-commu-
nism. While their lifestyle may seem radical, the point is that the
needs of the poorer members of the church were met by the gener-
osity of those better off.

**Question 10.** If people have problems responding to this question,
suggest possible aspects of everyday life which should be affected
by commitment to Christ: study habits, work patterns, church and
family relationships, moral standards.

**Question 11.** You may want to omit this question if you are doing
this study in one session. If you are doing the study in two sessions,
then open the second study with this question.

**Question 12.** It is interesting to note that the word "kept back" in verse 2 is the same word used in the account of Achan who kept for himself some of the spoils of Jericho which were to be handed over into the treasury of the Lord's house (see Josh 6:18-19; 7:1).

**Question 13.** Don't get overly involved in a discussion of their punishment. The important truth to recognize is the seriousness of sin. Be sure the group notices Peter's description of their sin in verse 9 as agreeing to "test the spirit of the Lord." It seems that Ananias and Sapphira were trying to see how much they could get away with.

**Question 14.** Don't feel that everyone should share as there are a series of more general application questions ahead. However, there may be someone who is particularly struck by the nature of Ananias' and Sapphira's sin and wants to respond personally at this point.

**Question 15.** Verse 4 makes it clear that they were not obligated to donate their money to the Christian community. Their sin lay in their attempted deception of the church.

**Question 17.** Although the illustration of Barnabas' life is limited to two verses, Luke is actually using the whole passage (4:46—5:12) to contrast the attitude of Barnabas with that of Ananias and Sapphira.

The following commentary helps to put the two parts of this passage into perspective: "The greater length of the story of Ananias and Sapphira should not lead to the conclusion that it is the important incident, the preceding section being merely an introduction to give it a setting; on the contrary, it is more likely that 4:32-35 describes the pattern of life, and is then followed by two illustrations, positive and negative, of what happened in practice" (I. Howard Marshall, *The Acts of the Apostles* [Grand Rapids, Mich.: Eerdmans, 1980]).

Ananias and Sapphira would probably see commitment as an adherence to some external set of religious observances. For Barnabas it would be more a matter of the heart.

**Question 18.** Consider this as a follow-up to the previous question. You might think of ways in which Christians today focus on external factors in gauging Christian commitment.

**Question 19.** Help group members to think of a comparable action relevant to their own Christian context. It might have nothing to do with finances. For example, it might mean sacrificing a significant portion of time in serving fellow believers.

### Study 3. Struggling with the World's Values. Psalm 73.

*Purpose:* To recognize the transience of the world's values and to reaffirm God's goodness in a seemingly unjust world.

**Question 1.** Encourage a few people to share their experiences. The incident could relate either to themselves or to other Christians they know.

**Question 2.** Keep the discussion brief and general since details will be discussed later in the study.

**Question 3.** Help people to see Asaph's honesty here. He admits that envy, and not a disinterested concern for injustice, is the cause of his bitterness.

**Question 5.** Encourage the group to be specific. Notice that every part of the mind and body has been affected.

**Question 7.** The Hebrew text of this verse is somewhat unclear, but most commentators feel it refers to the popular worship of success.

**Question 8.** Help group members to be concrete in their answers, but don't spend too much time on this question if it has already been covered in the discussion of question 1.

**Question 11.** Have an example ready if the group is having trouble answering this question.

**Question 12.** The group should see that the situation Asaph has been describing seems like a mockery of his statement in verse 1. God's goodness to Israel (his people) is *not* in fact evident in this passage. Asaph's assertion can only have been made from a perspective of faith.

**Question 13.** Allow several people to respond to this question. Be sure to pray about these circumstances in your closing time. You might want to skip this question if you are doing this study in one session.

**Question 14.** Use this question to open the second session if you are doing the study in two parts.

**Question 15.** If you are doing this study in two parts, have someone summarize Psalm 73:1-14 (the first part of the text) before reading the second half of the passage. The group should notice that Asaph has begun to look beyond himself, seeing the possible effects of his attitude on those around him.

**Question 16.** Several answers are possible. At the very least, help people see Asaph's sense of responsibility toward others which restrains him from openly expressing his feelings. Personal insights might be helpful, but don't let the discussion wander too far from the text.

**Question 17.** Verse 17 is the pivotal verse in the chapter. The "sanctuary" is the place of worship. Only as the psalmist turns to God himself in adoration is his vision cleared. Skip the second part of this question if it has already been answered in the preceding discussion.

**Questions 19-20.** Asaph's time in God's presence has changed his perspective not only on the wicked (vv. 18-20, see question 17) but also on his own attitude. You might want to note that there is an interesting progression in Asaph's assessment of his own attitude. In verse 2 he sees his attitude of envy as a danger to his own faith, that is, to himself personally. In verse 15 he views these feelings as potentially dangerous to his fellow believers. Finally, in verses 21-22 he considers his attitude as an affront to God himself.

**Question 21.** Notice the contrast between the wicked's claims to heaven and earth in verse 9 and Asaph's perspective in verse 25. For Asaph the claim that God was his portion (v. 26) was especially significant, for he was a Levite. In the allotment of the promised land (Josh 14:1-5), the Levites received no portion of it. They were supported by tithes and set apart for God as ministers of the tabernacle. God alone was their "portion."

**Question 23.** Help group members to focus on something specific, for example, Asaph's envy of the prosperous, his frustration with his own situation, or his transforming experience in worship.

**Study 4. Perseverance. Hebrews 10:19-39.**
*Purpose:* To understand the nature and cost of perseverance and to gain motivation to continue steadfastly in commitment to Christ.
**Question 1.** This question is intended as an introduction to the theme of the study and should not be discussed exhaustively. One or two examples from the personal experience of group members could be helpful here.
**Questions 2-3.** In verses 19-21, as throughout the book of Hebrews, the author is very conscious of the Jewish audience to which he is writing. Therefore he describes the Christian's approach to God within the framework of the Old Testament sacrificial system.

What is new and radical for these Jewish believers is the very possibility of direct access to God. Under the old covenant only the high priest could approach God on behalf of the people, and that only one day each year. Now, however, by the "new and living way"—the perfect sacrifice of Christ—believers can enter God's presence with the confidence that he will graciously receive them.

If the Old Testament background is covered in response to question 2, you may want to omit question 3.
**Question 4.** The exhortation in verse 22 uses liturgical phrases which are also taken from old covenant ritual. The four conditions for approaching God are "a sincere heart," "full assurance of faith," hearts cleansed of a guilty conscience, and "bodies washed with pure water." The reference to washing may be an allusion to baptism, a symbol of inward purity.
**Question 5.** There is an interesting progression in these verses: draw near, hold unswervingly, spur one another on, and do not give up meeting together. The exhortation to draw near to God seems to undergird the others. You need not enter into a lengthy discussion at this point, but the group should note that a close personal relationship with God is foundational to each command.

**Question 7.** This is a particularly important question. Be sure to allot sufficient time for it.

Group members should recognize our responsibility toward one another in the body of Christ and the importance of fellowship and mutual encouragement for perseverance in the Christian life. A few personal examples (positive or negative) illustrating these truths could be very helpful in driving home these points.

**Question 8.** Help group members to be practical here. Again, a few concrete examples would be valuable.

**Question 9.** The author points to the imminent return of Christ as a motivation to steadfastness. The admonition that the Day is approaching, however, also reminds us of the shortness and uncertainty of life in general.

If you are short on time, you may want to skip this question as the theme recurs in the second part of the study.

**Questions 10-11.** These verses warn us of potential dangers of neglecting Christian fellowship. It may eventually lead to a renunciation of faith with its grave consequences. See also Hebrews 6:4-8.

Don't let the discussion get bogged down on the possibility of losing one's salvation as this is not the focus of the study. (For various interpretations of this passage you might want to check a commentary. For suggestions see the list of supplementary readings.) Your discussion of question 10 may be extensive enough to warrant omitting question 11.

**Question 12.** Among the various practical steps which might be mentioned, be sure the importance of consistent fellowship is emphasized. The second part of the question should help in this regard.

**Question 13.** Use this question to open the second session if you are doing the study in two parts.

**Question 15.** As in the first half of the study the need for community is apparent. Be sure the group sees this as an important aspect of perseverance.

**Question 16.** This is a broad question. Help group members to focus on specifics, such as pressure at work or among peers.

**Question 17.** Encourage people to go beyond the idea of sympathizing, important as that may be. Consider what it might cost to identify with fellow Christians—in the US and overseas—who are being mistreated in some way.

**Question 18.** At least three factors should be mentioned: reward, God's faithfulness to his promises, and Christ's imminent return.

**Question 19.** The Old Testament citations are adapted from Isaiah 26:20 (v. 37) and Habakkuk 2:3-4 (v. 38). The writer wanted to emphasize the certainty of Christ's return. It seems that disappointment over the delay of Christ's Second Coming was one of the reasons why some believers fell away. The promised return of Christ should encourage all believers to hold fast to their commitment since there will indeed be an end to the trials and hardships of this life.

**Question 20.** In commenting on verse 39 John Calvin throws light on the stern warnings in this chapter of Hebrews. "Warnings and admonitions are the very means which God employs to secure the final salvation of His people; and to conclude from such warnings that they may finally fall away, is by no means a legitimate argument" (as quoted in Thomas Hewitt, *The Epistle to the Hebrews* [Grand Rapids, Mich.: Eerdmans, 1960]).

**Question 21.** One view of perseverance is not necessarily better than the other. Help people see that both aspects of perseverance are necessary.

**Question 23.** This final question is intended to focus again on the communal aspect of perseverance. Holding fast to the faith should be more than just a matter of personal struggle. We are called to mutual encouragement and responsibility.

### Study 5. Taking Risks. Numbers 13:1—14:9.

*Purpose:* To identify fears which inhibit our Christian growth and to resolve to trust God in at least one area of spiritual challenge.

**Question 1.** There is no need to elicit specific personal responses.

General areas such as sharing one's faith, relating to parents, or anxiety about the future might be discussed.

**Question 3.** Be sure the group recognizes that Moses commissioned the spies to find out both the obstacles and the benefits facing them in taking the land.

**Question 4.** Notice both what they did and where they went. It might be helpful to follow the spies' journey on a map.

**Question 6.** The fact that Caleb had to silence the people after the report was given suggests that their initial reaction was one of consternation or confusion.

**Question 9.** The group should see that the spies were commissioned to gather facts about the land they were going to enter. In verses 31-33 we find the spies no longer reporting observations, but rather *interpreting* the information they have collected. This probably reflects their fear.

**Question 10.** Caleb viewed the situation in light of God's promise. The perspective of the other spies seems to have been limited by what they saw physically.

**Question 11.** This question should help group members to think about how their fears affect their relationship with God. It may be skipped if you are pressed for time since answers to question 12 (another application question) may well cover this issue.

**Question 12.** Encourage people to share not only a "giant" in their life but also what it might mean to gain a renewed perspective on such a difficult situation they face. Be sure to pray for one another in response to what has been shared.

**Question 13.** Use this question to open the second session if you are doing the study in two parts. You should probably omit this question if you are doing the study in one session.

**Question 14.** If you are doing the study in two sessions, you may want to have someone summarize the first part of the study before reading the rest of the chapter.

Try to keep the discussion here on a general level, particularly focusing on the atmosphere in the camp.

**Questions 16-17.** The desire to return to Egypt is worth special consideration. It is a good example of the "play it safe" streak in most of us (which may have been discussed in question 13). The Israelites would rather return to the past, miserable as it was, than face the challenges of the unknown that lay before them. Some people in your group may be able to identify with such feelings.

**Question 19.** Their perspective in this situation is centered on God. Falling face down and tearing one's clothes were signs of humility before God.

**Question 20.** Notice in particular how Joshua and Caleb reverse the negative assessment of the spies in 13:32. While the spies feared the land would devour them, Joshua and Caleb claimed that with God's help the children of Israel would "swallow up" the people of the land (14:9). It is important to see that disobeying God would in fact be a greater risk than attempting to take the land.

**Question 22.** Obviously, stoning is not in fashion in most circles today, but Christians face risks such as ostracism, ridicule, and loss of a position or promotion at work.

**Question 23.** The first part of this question need not be interpreted negatively. It is certainly good to maintain consistency in habits, such as daily quiet time, prayer and other spiritual disciplines. However, group members should consider ways in which God may want to stretch them. Help people to think about new challenges in trusting God.

### Study 6. Faithfulness. Matthew 25:14-46.

*Purpose:* To recognize our God-given abilities and resources and to seek ways to use them in Christ's service.

**Question 1.** The purpose of this question is to stimulate thought concerning the use of our resources. Avoid a lengthy discussion about the particulars of financial investment. Help group members consider other areas of investment, such as time, children and other material possessions.

**Question 2.** This parable is the second in a series of three parables of judgment in chapter 25. Commonly known as the parable of the "talents," the story is not concerned with natural human abilities we normally designate as talents.

**Question 3.** The master knows his servants and what they are capable of. This is the basis of his allotment. If this fact has already been noted in your discussion of question 2, skip it.

**Question 5.** Make sure the group does not treat this question superficially. There are a number of lessons to be learned from the master's response.

**Question 7.** It is important for the group to recognize that the servant's action was based on a misconception of his master's character. But even with this misconception he should have been all the more enterprising with the money entrusted to him. The servant seems to have regarded faithfulness as a static quality. He treats the money as a dead object and therefore buries it. At the very least the servant should have deposited the money in a bank to earn "interest" (v. 27). It is interesting to note that the Greek word used here for interest, *tokos,* means offspring, thereby denoting something living rather than dead.

**Questions 8-9.** The master's response to the third servant highlights the seriousness of the call to faithfulness. The money that the servant buried was not his own. It had been entrusted to him by the master, and his failure to use it was a serious breach of confidence.

**Question 10.** Excuses might include lack of time, feelings of inadequacy ("I don't have any talents") and fear of failure.

**Question 11.** In addition to being pleased by the faithfulness of the first two servants, the master rewards them with greater responsibility. You may want to discuss the nature of this reward since increased responsibility may seem to be more of a burden than a joy for some people in your group.

**Question 12.** Encourage group members to focus not only on conspicuous natural abilities but to see their spiritual gifts, resources and even character traits as "talents" entrusted to them by God.

**Question 14.** This question is only meant to help people enter into the passage. As the question raises a controversial issue, you might want to limit the question to a few responses. Don't let it get out of hand. You'll get a chance to return to this issue at the end of the study.

**Question 15.** This parable describes the final judgment. For other scriptural references to this event see Matthew 16:27 and Ezekiel 34:17-34. You also might want to note that this is the only place in the Gospels where Christ refers to himself, "the Son of man," as King. In addition to observing the general setting, be sure group members mention the various people involved in the proceedings.

**Question 18.** The gravity of sins of omission is underscored by the fact that it is condemned both here and in the preceding two parables. Just as the ten virgins are excluded for their failure to keep watch (25:1-13), and the third servant is punished for doing nothing with what was entrusted to him, so the goats are condemned for their negligence in serving others.

**Question 19.** The group should note that while the sheep and the goats pose precisely the same questions in response to the king's pronouncement, their underlying attitudes are vastly different. The sheep's response shows their unaffected humility and unself-consciousness in serving others. By means of the same questions, however, the goats attempt to excuse themselves for failing to serve.

**Question 22.** This is an open-ended question which reflects back on introductory question 14. Again, don't let the discussion wander too far from the passage. By now the group should realize that this chapter emphasizes the call to *faithfulness* in following Christ. But this does not supersede the primacy of *faith* in Christ.

**Questions 23-24.** Encourage group members to be practical and concrete in answering these questions. Feel free to skip question 24 if specific measures of application have already been discussed in response to question 23.

# For Further Reading

Aharoni, Yohanan, and Michael Avi-Yonah. *The Macmillan Bible Atlas.* New York: Macmillan, 1977.

Alexander, Donald L., ed. *Christian Spirituality: Five Views of Sanctification.* Downers Grove: InterVarsity Press, 1988.

St. Augustine. *City of God.* 7 vols. Loeb Classical Library. Harvard: Harvard University Press.

Bellah, Robert N., et al. *Habits of the Heart.* Berkeley, Calif.: University of California Press, 1985.

Bonhoeffer, Dietrich. *The Cost of Commitment.* New York: Macmillan, 1963.

Bonhoeffer, Dietrich. *Life Together.* San Francisco: Harper and Row, 1976.

Bright, John. *A History of Israel,* 3d ed. Philadelphia: Westminster Press, 1981.

Bunyan, John. *Pilgrim's Progress.* Moody Classics. Chicago, Ill.: Moody Press, 1984.

Buttrick, George Arthur, gen. ed. *The Interpreter's Bible in Twelve Volumes.* New York and Nashville: Abingdon Press, 1954.

Comenius, J. A. *The Labyrinth of the World and the Paradise of the Heart.* Ann Arbor: University of Michigan, 1972.

Douglas, J. D. *The New Bible Dictionary.* Grand Rapids, Mich.: Eerdmans, 1962.

Ferguson, Sinclair B., and David F. Wright, eds. *New Dictionary of Theology.* Downers Grove: InterVarsity Press, 1988.

Friesen, Gary, and Robin Maxson. *Decison Making and the Will of God.* Portland, Ore.: Multnomah, 1985.

Gasque, W. Ward, ed. New International Greek Commentary. Grand Rapids, Mich.: Eerdmans, 1978-.

Godet, Frederick Louis. *Commentary on Romans.* Grand Rapids, Mich.: Kregel, 1977.

Guthrie, D., J. A. Motyer, A. M. Stibbs, D. J. Wiseman. *The New Bible Commentary, Revised.* Grand Rapids, Mich.: Eerdmans, 1970.

Havel, Vaclav. *The Power of the Powerless.* M. E. Sharpe, 1990.

Hodge, Charles. *Romans.* Edinburgh: The Banner of Truth Trust, 1972.

Hodge, Charles. *Systematic Theology.* Grand Rapids, Mich.: Eerdmans, 1981.

Hubbard, Robert L., Jr. *The Book of Ruth.* The New International Commentary on the Old Testament. Grand Rapids, Mich.: Eerdmans, 1988.

Kuhatschek, Jack. *Taking the Guesswork out of Applying the Bible.* Downers Grove, Ill.: InterVarsity Press, 1990.

Keil, C. F., and F. Delitzsch. *Commentary on the Old Testament in Ten Volumes.* Grand Rapids, Mich.: Eerdmans, 1980.

Kierkegaard, Søren. *Fear and Trembling.* Books on Demand UMI.

Lewis, C. S. *The Screwtape Letters.* Rev. ed. New York: Macmillan, 1982.

Lewis, C. S. *Surprised by Joy.* New York: Harcourt, Brace & World, 1955.

Luther, Martin. *Freedom of the Christian.*

Morris, Leon. *The Gospel According to St. Luke.* New Testament Commentaries. Grand Rapids, Mich.: Eerdmans, 1974.

Nicholas, Ron, et al. *Good Things Come in Small Groups.* Downers Grove, Ill.: InterVarsity Press, 1985.

Nicholas, Ron, et al. *Small Group Leaders' Handbook.* Downers Grove, Ill.: InterVarsity Press, 1981.

Nyquist, James, and Jack Kuhatschek. *Leading Bible Discussions.* Downers Grove: InterVarsity Press, 1985.

Nystrom, Carolyn. *Romans: Christianity on Trial.* Wheaton, Ill.: Harold Shaw, 1980.

Nystrom, Carolyn, and Matthew Floding. *Relationships: Face to Face.* Wheaton, Ill.: Harold Shaw, 1986.

Peterson, Eugene. *A Long Obedience in the Same Direction.* Downers Grove, Ill.: InterVarsity Press, 1980.

Plueddemann, Jim and Carol. *Pilgrims in Progress.* Wheaton: Harold Shaw, 1990.

Smith, Blaine. *Knowing God's Will.* Rev. ed. Downers Grove, Ill.: InterVarsity Press, 1991.

Tenney, Merrill C., gen. ed. *The Zondervan Pictoral Encyclopedia of the Bible.* Grand Rapids, Mich.: Zondervan, 1976.

Tyndale New Testament Commentaries. Grand Rapids, Mich.: Eerdmans.

Wesley, John and Charles. *Selected Prayers, Hymns, Journal Notes, Sermons, Letters and Treatises.* New York: Paulist Press, 1981.

White, John. *Magnificent Obsession.* Downers Grove, Ill.: InterVarsity Press, rev. 1990.

## Christian Character Bible Studies from InterVarsity Press
*in 6 or 12 studies for individuals or groups*

**Deciding Wisely** by Bill Syrios. Making tough decisions is part of life. Through these Bible studies, you'll find out how to pray for God's will, listen to his voice and become a wise person. These principles of godly decision-making will enable you to serve God in the decisions you make. 1148-6.

**Finding Contentment** by Carolyn Nystrom. The contentment that characterizes the Christian life is found in intangibles—trust, love, joy, comfort and hope. The studies in this guide will introduce you to these keys to complete fulfillment in Christ. 1145-1.

**Living in the World** by Carolyn Nystrom. How do we glorify God in secular work? How should we spend our money? What kind of political involvement should we have? This guide is designed to help us clarify godly values so that we will not be affected by the warped values of the world. 1144-3.

**Loving God** by Carolyn Nystrom. Studies on how God loves—and how his gracious and stubborn love provide the foundation for our love for him. As we learn to love God as he loves us, we'll learn how to be more who he wants us to be. 1141-9.

**Loving One Another** by Carolyn Nystrom. This guide will help you to solve your differences with other Christians, learn to worship together, encourage one another and open up to each other. Discover the bond of love between believers that is a joyful tie! 1142-7.

**Loving the World** by Carolyn Nystrom. God has created a glorious world. Our responsibility is to help preserve and protect it. From valuing the sanctity of life to sharing your faith to helping the oppressed to protecting the environment, these Bible studies will help you discover your role in God's creation. 1143-5.

**Pursuing Holiness** by Carolyn Nystrom. Character traits such as honesty, self-control, sexual purity and integrity may seem out of date. Yet, God's will for us is that we live holy lives. Through Christ, we can find the strength we need to live in a way that glorifies God. These studies will help you to pursue the traits of holiness. 1147-8.

**Staying Faithful** by Andrea Sterk Louthan and Howard Louthan. This study guide is about wholehearted commitment to Christ. We will be motivated not only to persevere in Christ, but also to grow by taking the risks that will allow us to move forward in our Christian lives. Discover the power of faithfulness! 1146-X.

*Andrea Sterk Louthan and Howard Louthan live in Princeton, NJ, where they are doctoral candidates in church history and history respectively. Andrea is also the coauthor of the best-selling LifeGuide®* Bible Studies *Christian Character* and *Christian Disciplines* (IVP).